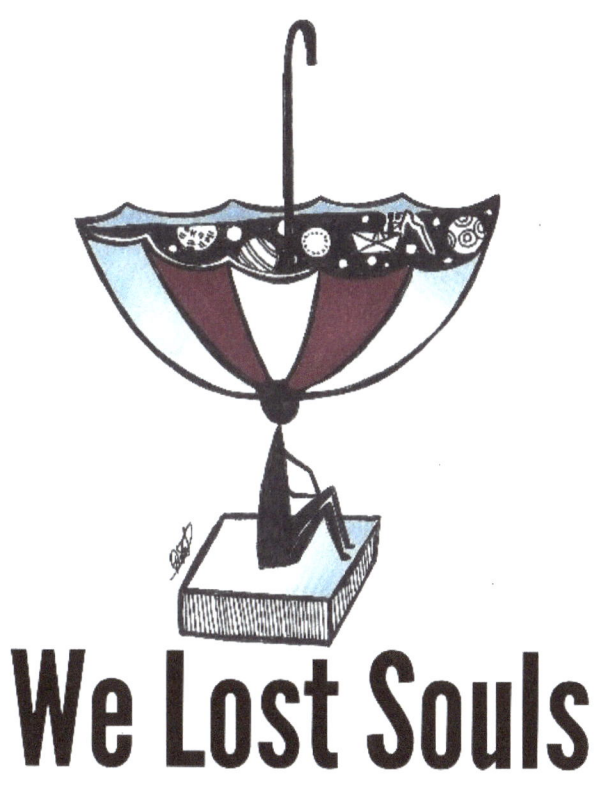

We Lost Souls

Volume 1

Copyright 2019

Copyright (c) 20109 by We Lost Souls. All rights reserved. This book or any portion thereof may not be reproduced or used in any manner whatsoever without the express written permission of the authors, except for the use of brief quotations in a book review.
Printed in the United States of America.
First Printing, 2019

Table Of Contents

adisorderedmindzine	Pg 4
artyprose	Pg 5
pianoetry	Pg 6, 41, 42
bbsartwork	Pg 7, 17, 24, 29, 34
floretstars	Pg 9
bipolarbear_art	Cover art, Pg 10
storieslikestars	Pg 11
arthasfeeling	Pg 12
my_troubled_art	Pg 13, 14
annaxmania	Pg 15, 22, 30
roman_empyre	Pg 16
redlightwriting	Pg 18
artful_agony	Pg 19
robertjw4688	Pg 20, 28
colette.lh	Pg 21, 31
morethanmagnets	Pg 23
just-4-thought	Pg 25
pi.and.anne	Pg 26
drixkie	Pg 27
_ohmycas	Pg 32
nefarious.psyche	Pg 33, 37
rainbow__ink	Pg 35
stones_poetry	Pg 36
inebriating_society	Pg 38, 39
ampoetry_	Pg 40
teacup__13	Pg 41, 42
iridesenceofbeing	Pg 43
sandyplottke	Pg 8, 44

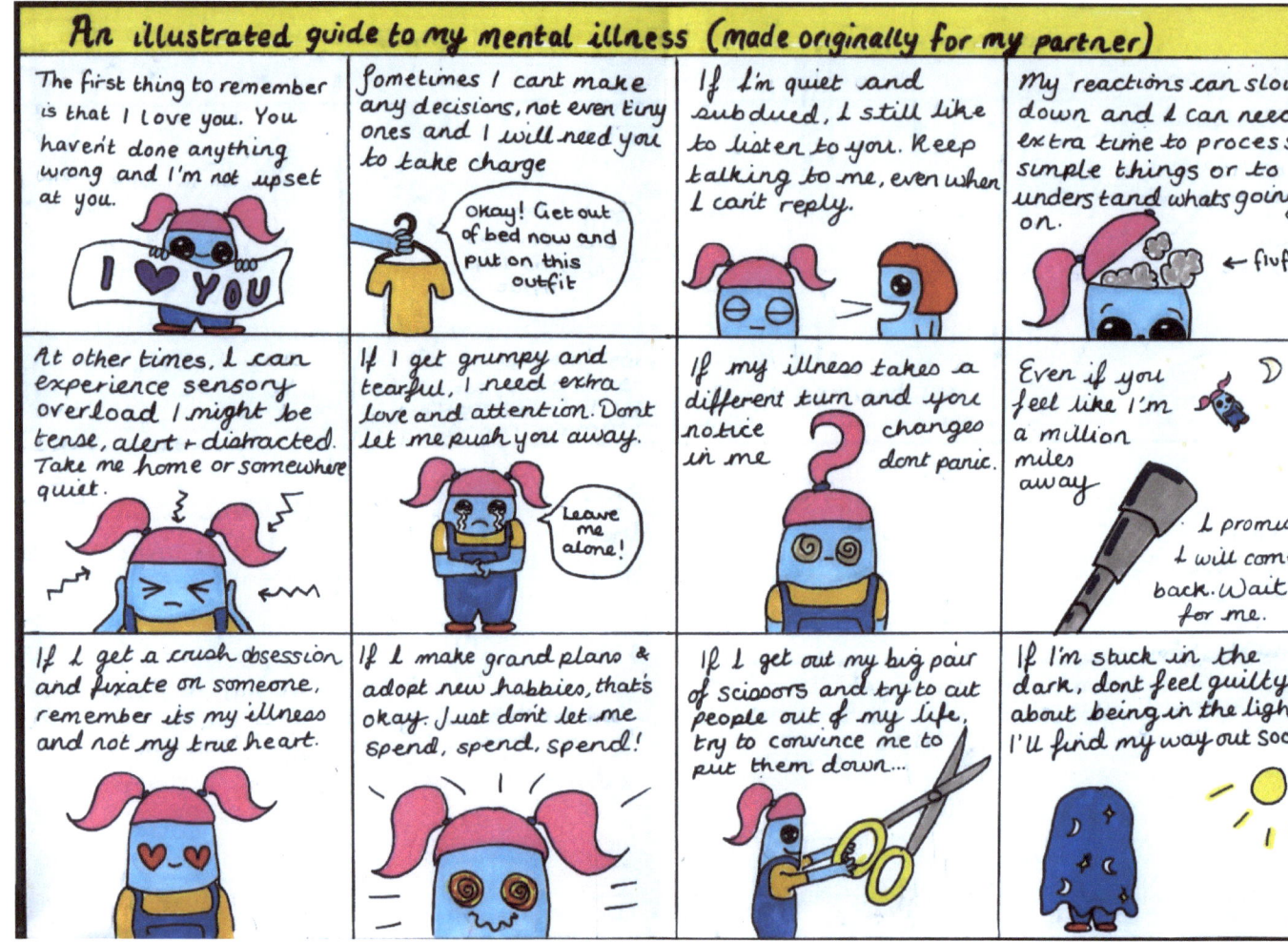

@adisorderedmindzine

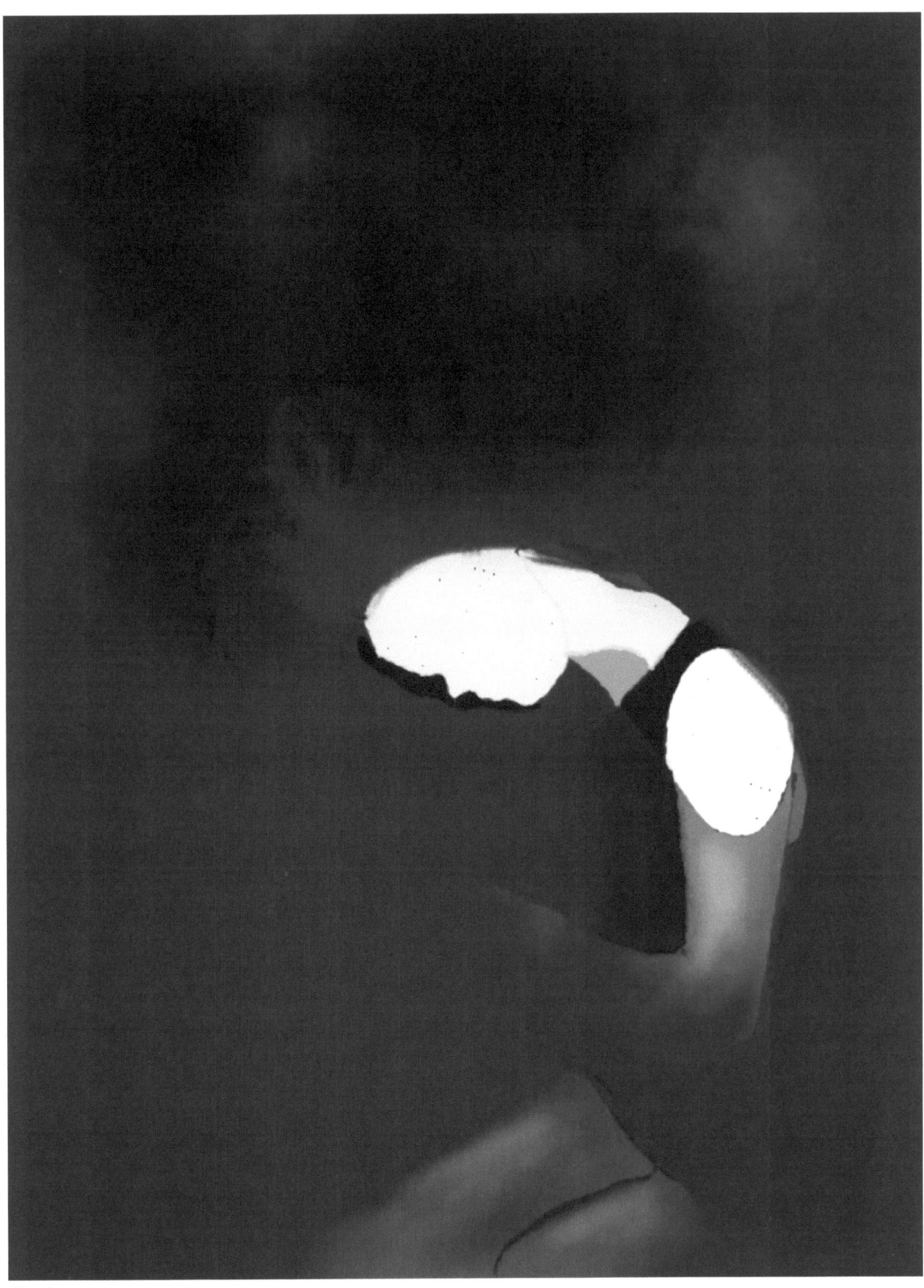

@artyprose

mental illness.

my writing isn't always happy, so my depression has a poetic facade— hidden underneath a pile of love letters that I will never read out love, we're all addicted to something or someone. we all need someone or something to make us smile. I've been finding out the truth as I age. you're never going to grow if you don't outgrow your bad habits. sometimes I feel like I'm in a shootout with myself and my demons have held me hostage. I'm all gassed up and I can't stop laughing. my worst fears come to life when the nightmares keep me up, so I try not to sleep. sometimes when I feel lonely, I write for people because that way, they won't feel what I feel. and I think writing is probably my most positive habit, even if it's kinda depressing. it helps people. but… I guess it could be looked at as a bad habit too. I have to keep digging and digging just to write how I might feel if I was said person. like right now, I know about bad habits. so I don't have to imagine what smoking is doing to you because I know the coughing is fucking you up and your lungs are as dark as they come, you've been a human volcano for so long, the dinosaurs are afraid that you'll erupt. I've sewn my lips shut and lit a fire so deep inside of myself that the smoke doesn't have anywhere to escape, but deeper into a hell designed by my own hands. I'm probably not the best person to ask about bad habits, but maybe admitting that fact makes me the best person to tell you the truth.

baby, here's the deal. I know that you're all messed up and smoking helps. but at the rate that you're going. you're going to die young. that's the truth. your truth and my truth as well. I know that I have to give up the drugs and the cigarettes or I won't make it. that's all that we really want, right? peace of mind. have you tried everything? meditation? picking up a hobby? learning a new language? learning how to play an instrument? figuring out how to make a thousand dollars in an hour? have you tried everything else, but smoking? the answer is probably no. why not give those other options a go? I'm a hypocrite, but I am also aware. but I think, you are too. so I have faith in you and I'm proud of you for making it this far. this is your world, I'm just a writer that doesn't know any better. but you? you can change the world.

@pianoetry

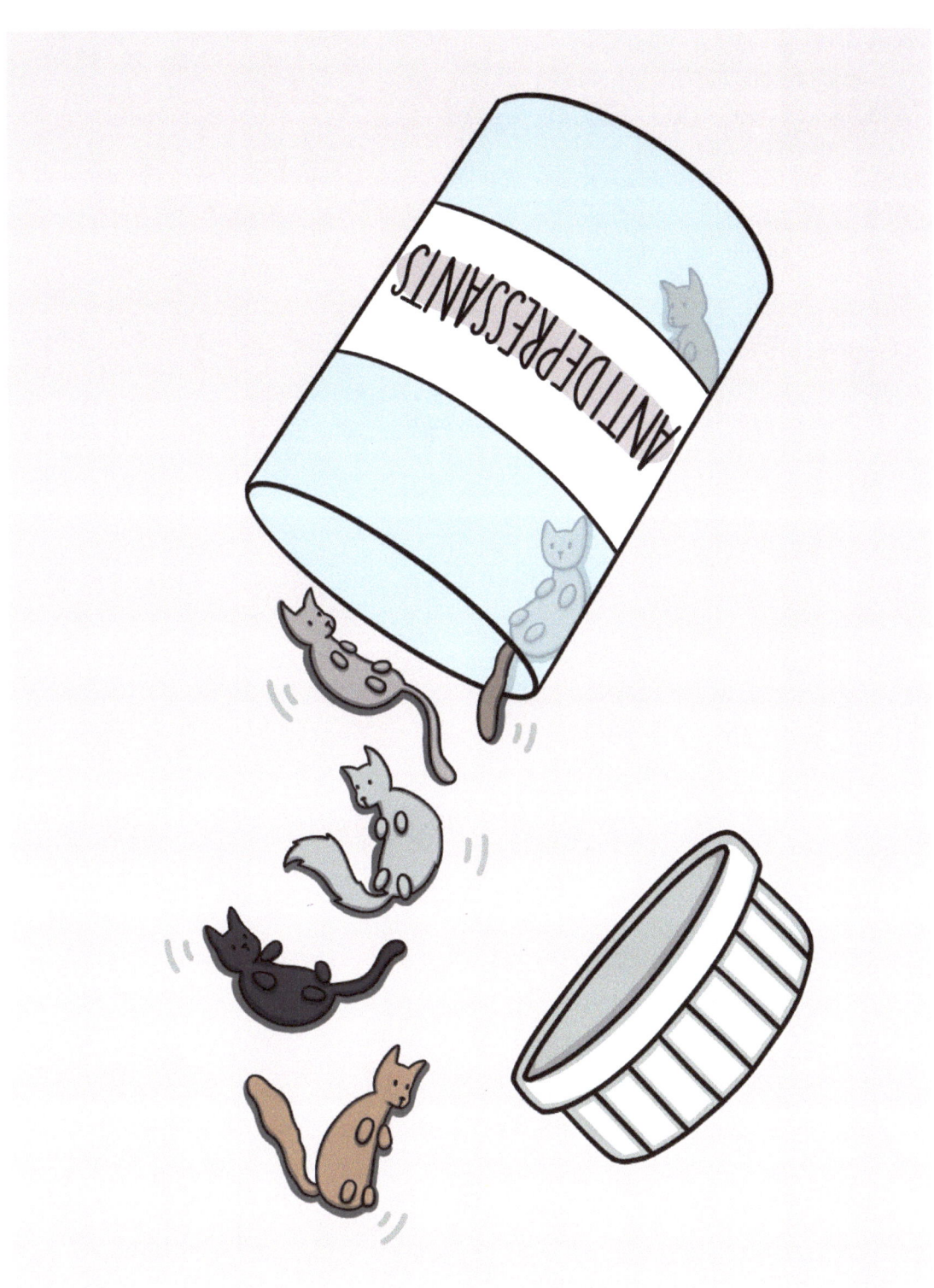

@bbsartwork

It took one person to notice
To notice that something's not right
It took one person to say something
To ask directly what was wrong

One single person.
And I didn't even know that person

One person to give me a small glimpse of hope
One person to tell me that I'm not alone
It took one person to show others that they can say something
One person to move more people to do the same
One person to save my life

@sandyplottke

NARRATOLOGY OF ME

call me angry & flushed -   tragic & wanton -
    Ophelia who drank the river - Lady Macbeth as a teenage girl -
    cause aren't all the sick girls just martyrs for the plot?
        defined by that one scene of madness,   that one Joan of Arc passion that
    strings you up onto the stake &   pulls the flames out of your lungs.
    they need to see the flames you hold to believe them.
what use is this poetry but to try & take away some of the burn?
            what use are words if not to name the wound?
        my wound: i am sick, black smoke trapped in the ache of
    my bones. i am sick, one cry for help poem after another.
call me girl found lost at the end of summer & one closed laceration of grief after another.

@floretstars

@bipolarbear_art

———

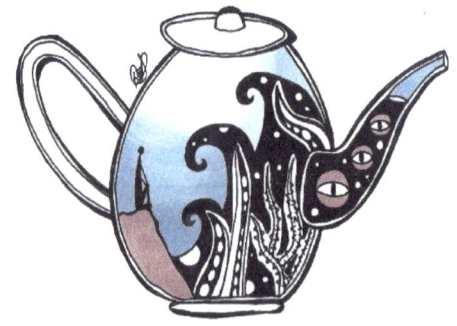

I write scars on my skin.
Call each streak a verse or a line if you will.
Dad didn't call back today. I shouldn't be surprised.　S t r i k e　1.
Mom gets sicker every day. She coughed blood again.　S t r i k e　2.
Still no sign of Dad. This is probably why he left. I was probably his sin.
Useless. Worthless. This is wishing. This is failing.
Oh, this is nothing.
S t r i k e 3.
S t r i k e 4.
This silence is loud, screaming against the cavern.
Pain is the only remedy to dull out the noise.
These lines are the only constant thing.

Strike—

nicole g | @storieslikestars

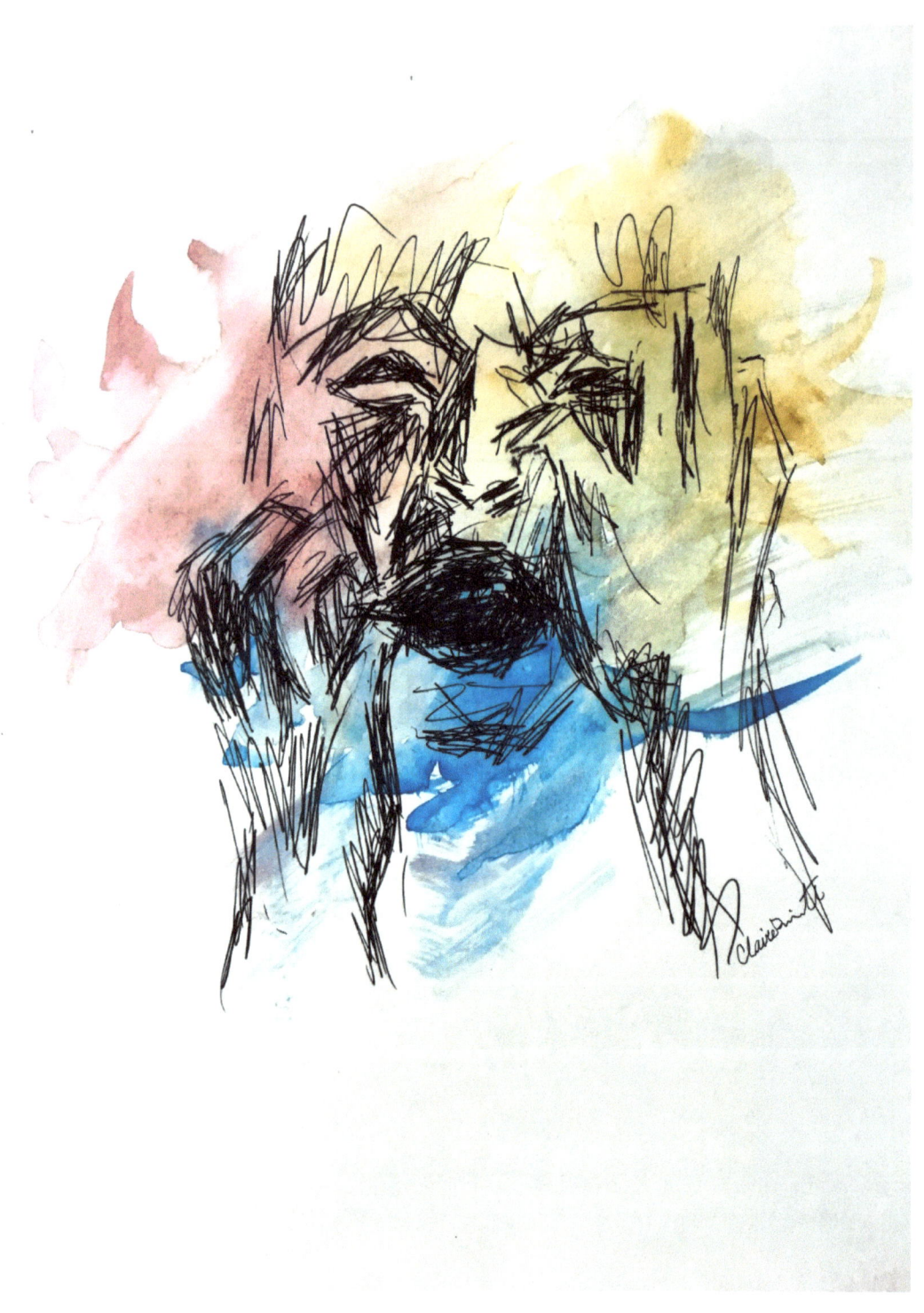

@art_has_feeling

"Why it's hard to get out of bed"

It's a veil, my friend.

A veil that covers my entire world.

Everything's fine.

Really, it is.

It's just that it all seems a little off.

Because the sky is just as blue,
The birdsong is still just as melodic,
The world is still as vibrant as ever.

But, i'm not.

Anhedonia pumps through my veins,
Settling into my bones.

And I don't know what to do.

I just can't get a grip.

Because my passion has been bound in chains;
Buried beneath the earth.

My heart has been hollowed out;
With cracks to let loose anything that tries to live in it.

My reality is disjointed.

I can't tell what's real sometimes.

And when my face cracks is that just a misinterpretation or is it a mask falling away?

Is this even my real face?

Do I have a real face?

It's been so long that I can't always tell.

But, the fire doesn't die;
No matter what harsh winds blow.

Despite all things that try to snuff it out, my embers will flare again.

And though this depression is a lifelong companion with it's clawed hand wrapped around my throat, I will march forward.

Because I refuse to let even such a formidable foe as this kill me.

@my_troubled_art

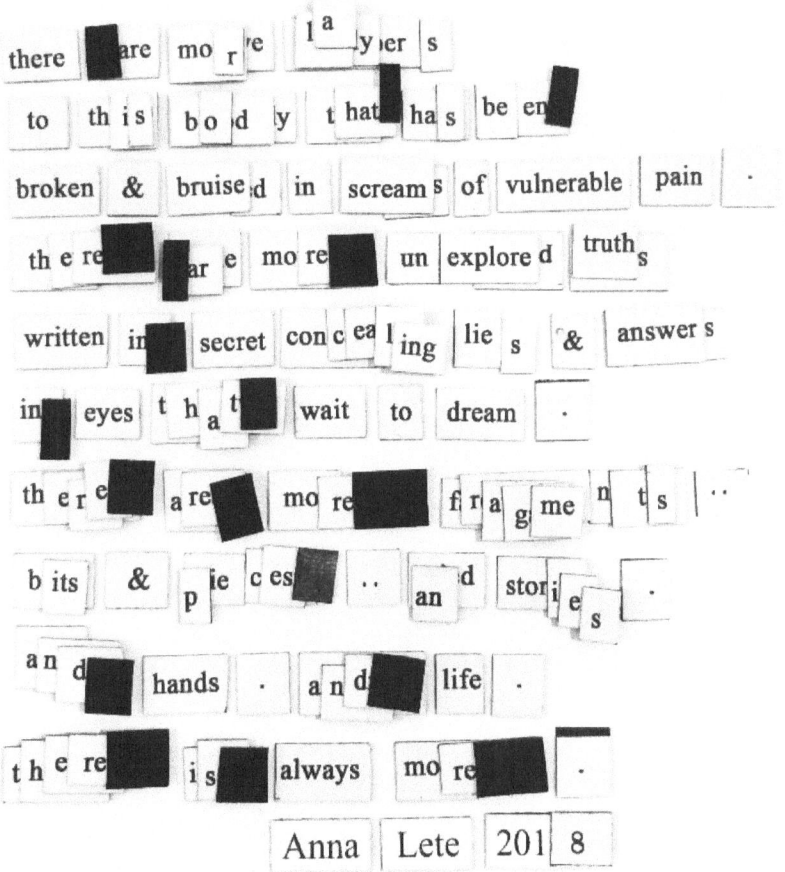

@annaxmania

"Apprehension" -A poem about anxiety

Each time the wound begins to,

Heal I take hold of a scalpel and;

I reopen the stitches to examine the.

Depth and scar tissue, reminding me;

Of the facets of the occurrences leading,

To the engraved marks that cover my mind;

Unable to break free from the vivid images,

That I have forcibly placed, inside my skull;

From analyzing the different angles within,

A meticulous manner that has continued;

To deepen the injury and cause it to be,

More remembered, than would of been;

Had I not obsessed and continuously saw,

The tissue that contained the memories that;

Formed along the surface of my entity until I,

Realize that the reason why, I was not moving;

Away from these moments is due to the constant,

Fixation on what could not be changed instead of;

Learning from the trauma, I caused the damage,

Due to the persistence that was based on my;

Apprehension.

@roman—empyre

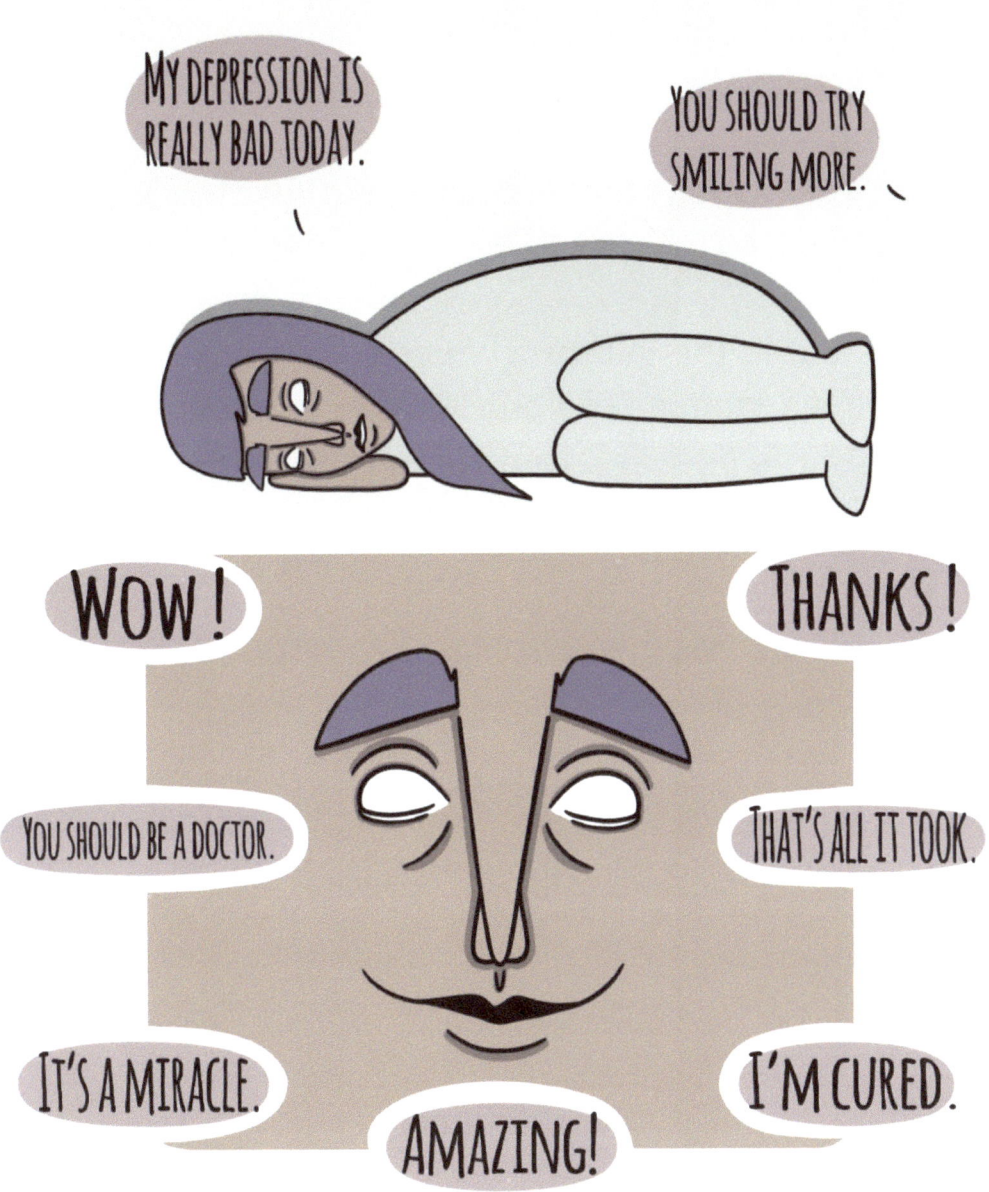

@bbsartwork

Stockholm Syndrome;

You can always tell when she crosses my mind.

I get very quiet, start mixing up my words &, I seclude.

I go back to the submissive state of mind that I escaped from. Like you're about to walk around the corner & remind me that I'm nothing.

I become nothing.

@redlightwriting

today's anxiety

brought to you by…

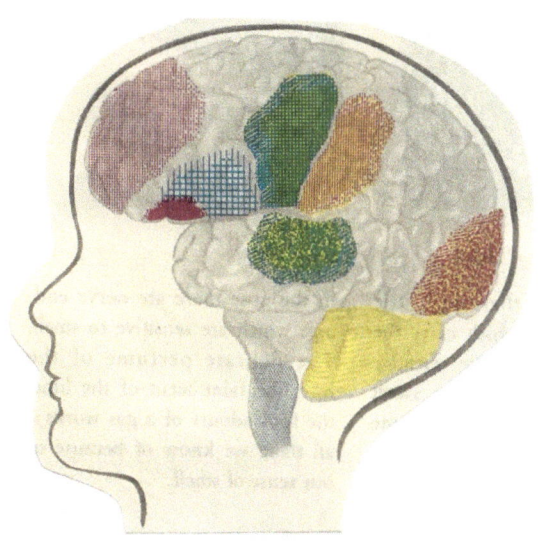

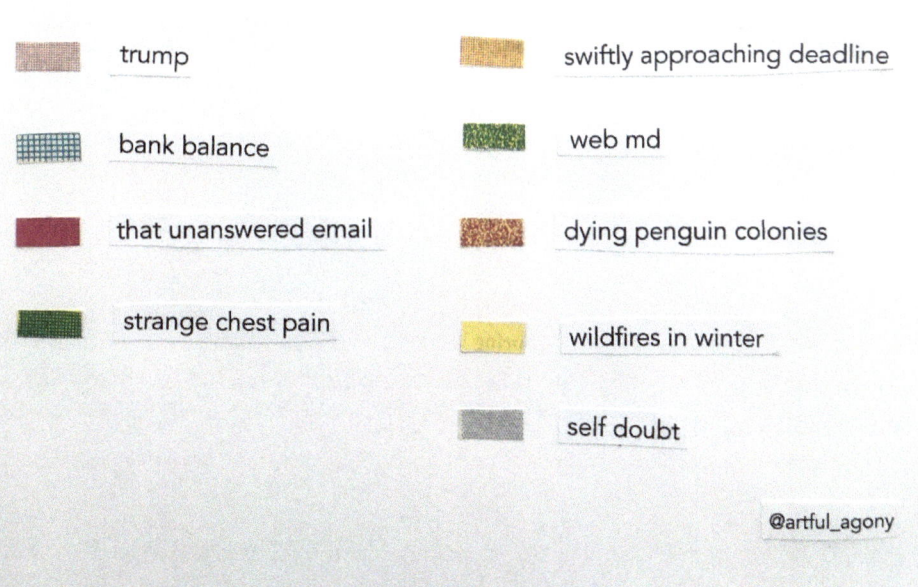

@artful_agony

"Panic Attack #4,688"

I'm shivering through
reality itself as
the alarms dance in
my head.
All synapses rage against
life; at war with
themselves, all
matter, and
lack thereof.
I try breathing in the
atmosphere to
slow my
machine-gun heart.
It slows but
still fires.
The planet will be
riddled with
bullet holes once
this is over and
I'm sorry.
I never wanted to be
an anxious mid-air
collision but
parts of me will
rain down
forever.
Don't try to
catch them.
The burn marks will
never heal.

@robertjw4688

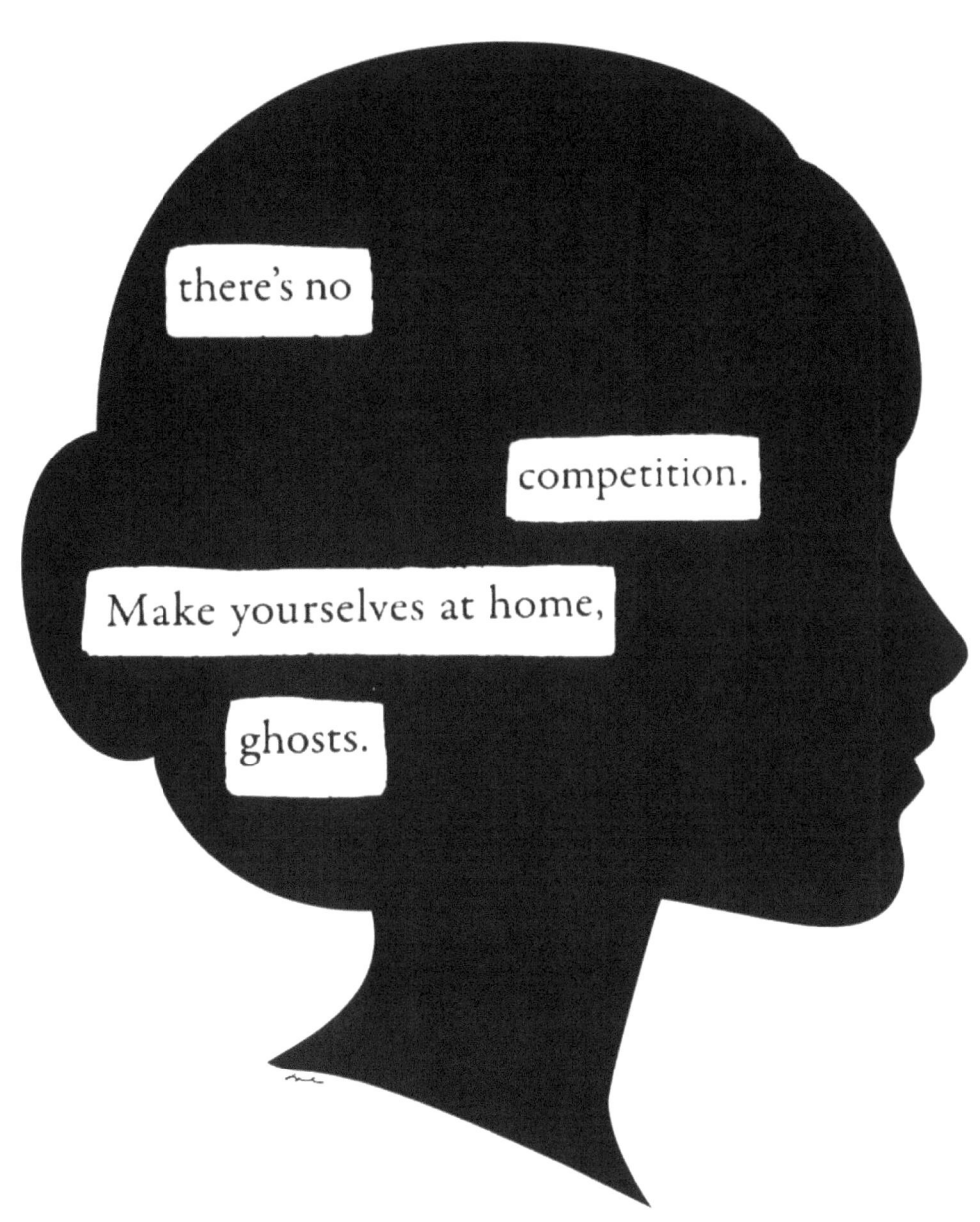

@colette.lh

@annaxmania

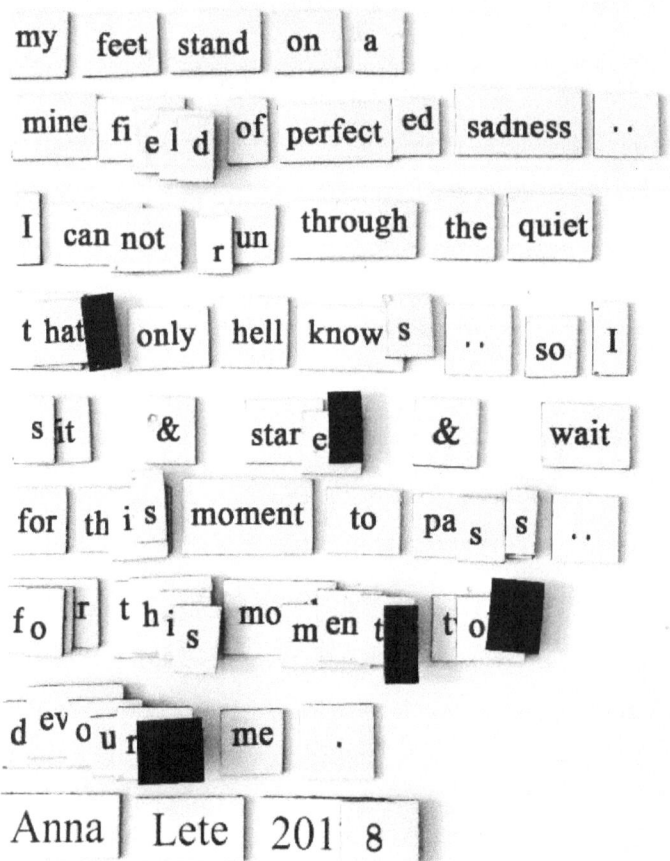

Some feel love.

Some feel fear creeping
up the slippery slope when the clouds cast shadows
onto the ground.

Some feel pain
echoing through the hollow tree
with the singing leaves, slowly swinging.

Some feel shame
sending ripples through the patchwork roots
woven 'round shallow soil that vibrates quietly.

Some feel the ache of want
unfold in the dark above the need
which pulls at the light-lined thread of hidden things.

When it stops, some feel guilt
gliding swiftly through the stark night sky that weeps
sweet sounds whimpering away.

Drips of rain
mark the way from the sun-baked book
to the eyes of those they fall from.
The whispers of wishes echo through the sounds of springs and rivers.
Must I ignore the call to sleep so as to not slip
into the world where familiar arms are waiting?

You can try to leave before the painted swirls in the stars serve
the darkest part of time and tire.

And imagine. How I cannot have the warmth
I desire.

How I cannot reach across any distance with my fingertips to touch
what I cannot see.

@morethanmagnets

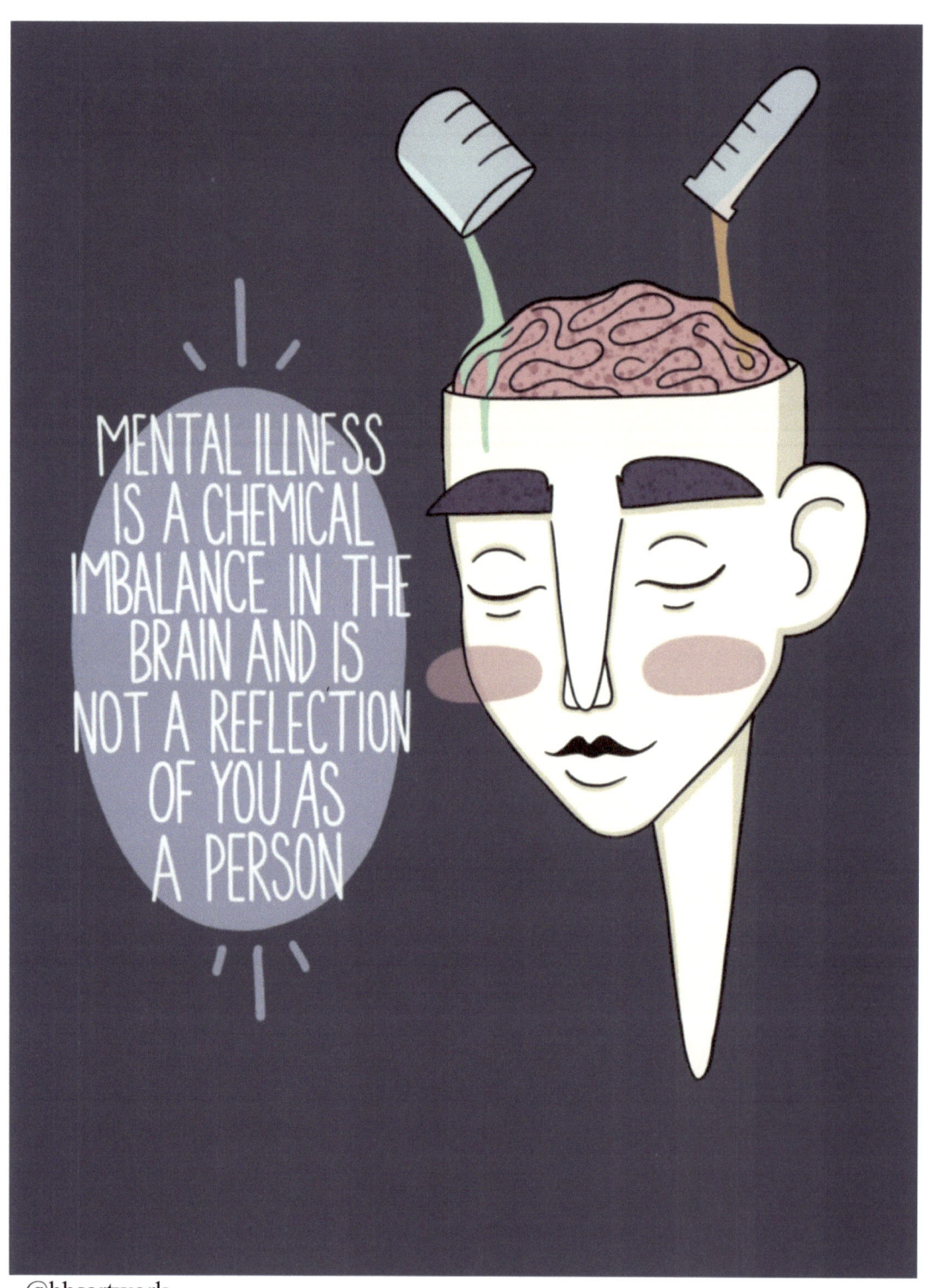

@bbsartwork

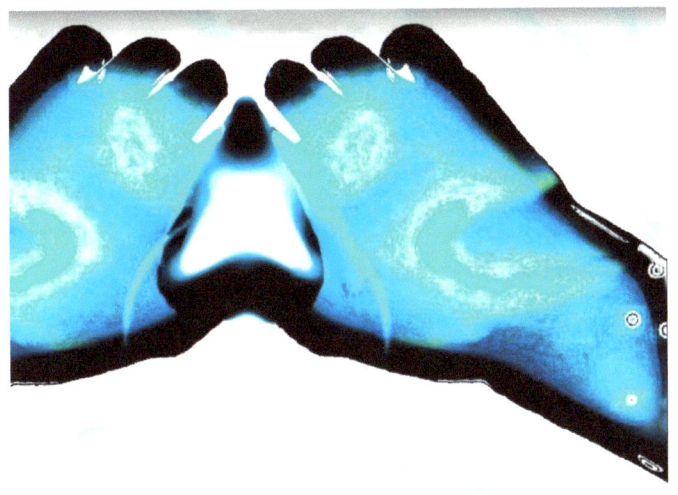

Breaking,
synonymous with living,
is where we find our home.
Petaled in this shelter,
I reach for no one.
For no one
is here
but the whisper
of my own breath,
begging for some path
laid with pavement
instead of the cobbled
stone, broken
and eroded.
I walk sharp edges.
I climb jagged cliffs.
If my path be treacherous,
then I shall be my guide,
then I shall bare my muscle,
and lift my body
from this hoveled hole,
then I shall wrench each step
as if walking towards my throne.

@just-4-thought

i wake up in the night and want to die
> **i do not want to die**

but no one asked when i was born
> **like this, so do i want to live,**

asked if i wanted to exist, asks if
> **i keep it, my old promise, my responsibility**

i fear, what happens when i overrule my core belief
> **not to hurt me or anybody in this world**

and my self-worth tries to outweigh
> **as good as i am able to**

but ends in a deep longing for no fight
> **when i wake up and want to die.**

the emptiness during the night.
> **remember, 'simply wait' is not a lie.**

pi & anne

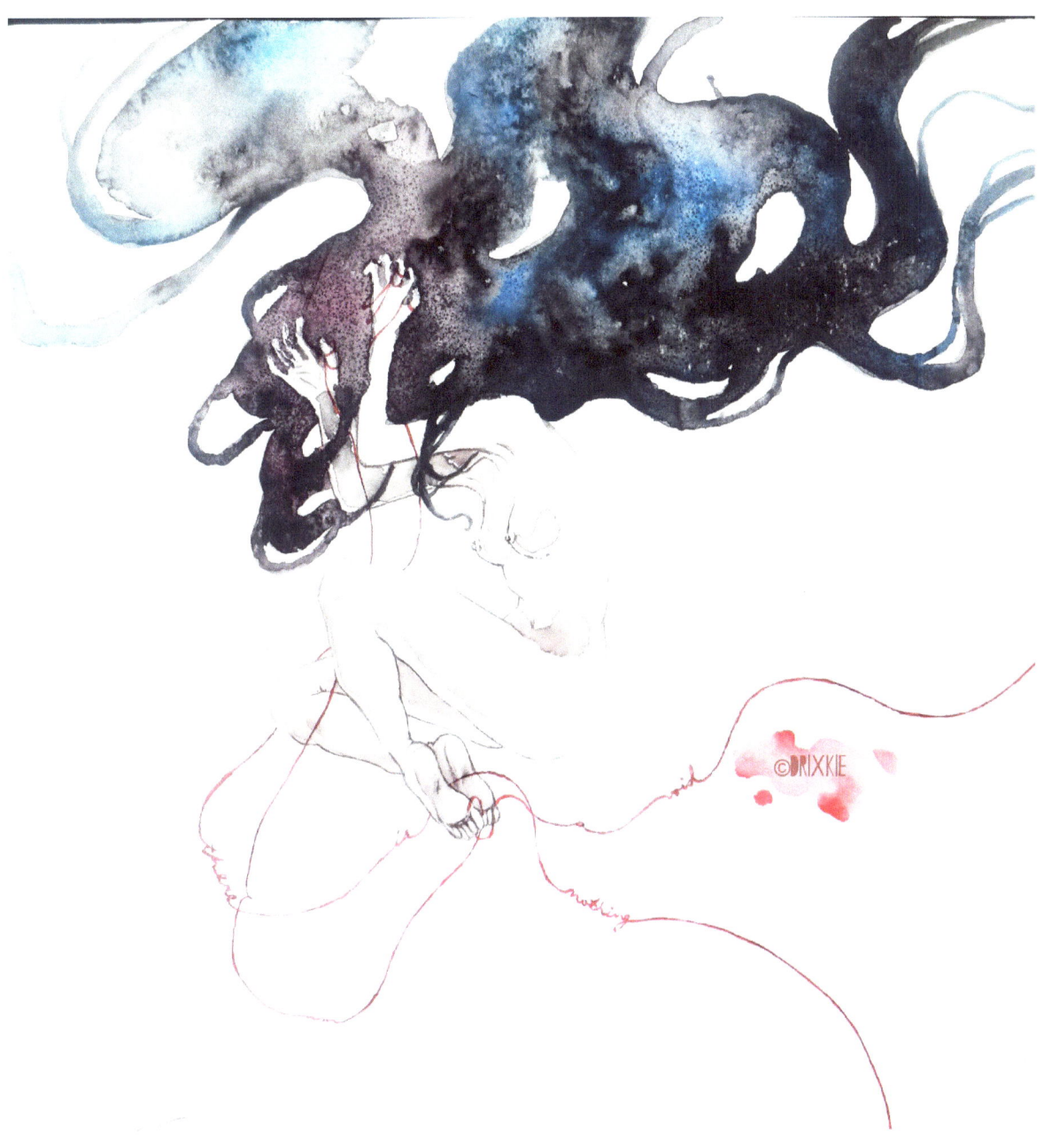

@drixkie

"Ghost Towns"

I see
ghost towns in every
reflective surface by which
I stumble.
Depression is
sleeping in the
Earth's core, dragging
my limbs
down
like a
captain-less ship.
Pill nights keep me
tame but
the beasts still
claw inside my
veins, leading to
coffin mornings.
I'm fighting with
both arms dangling
by their
nerve endings but
I know I'll
win someday
by perseverance alone.
I just need to
keep standing with my
body suspended by
music notes and
stray words, hanging
in the air like
halos over my head.

@robertjw4688

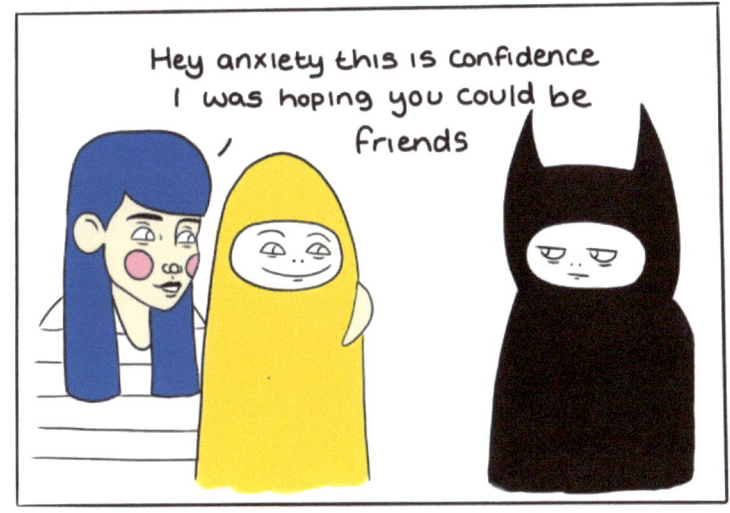
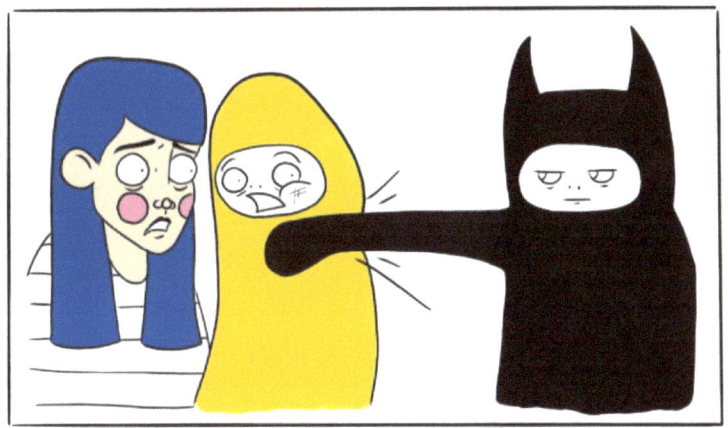
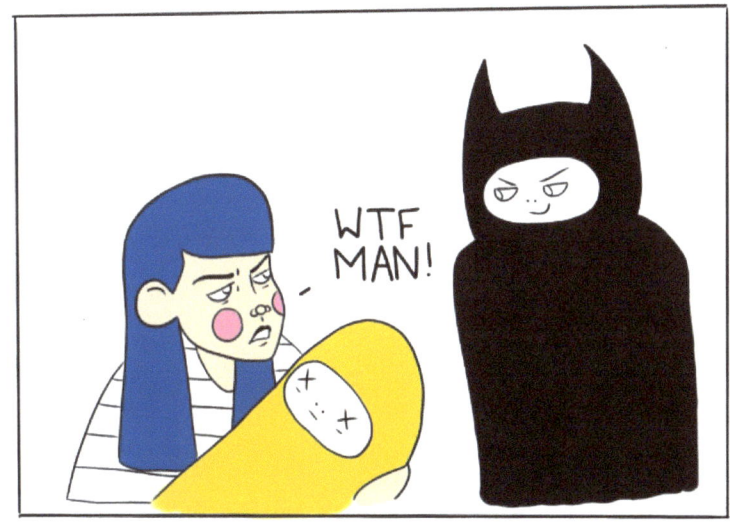

@bbsartwork

there is this space
broken yet perfected by distance
where you & I meet to drown
the wounded pieces of ourselves in hands
still desperately screaming .. speaking ..
offering anything .. everything . . so that
we might conquer life together .

Anna Lete 2018

@annaxmania

the Sun is

spending time alone.

so

the cold Winter,

still,

screams.

inside

our heads.

@colette.lh

There are ghosts that appear

to haunt and taunt your fears,
demonic figures will come to
play along and fiddle at your sorrow.
If you feel like singing then
allow the creation of a dark song.
Sink into the inadequate frequency
but once you have hung your woes
up on instruments of the damned;
please come back to the living dream,
recite the verses that allowed you to fight away Hell within, to the burning Sun.
Pause.
Stare your own reflection
into regal wisdom certifying
that each gloriously melodic scar
is a small token of another battle won.

-Cas.

@_ohmycas

BODY DRAIN

I soak my body in the ocean and hope it will drain
Salt should cause my cells to burst
Tissue should break
And I should lose weight

Every morning I look down
I see this layer of fat kissing my belly
Refusing to leave my thighs
I just want to suck it all out and breathe

My mum stores grains of salt in a glass
Hidden behind coffee in the corner cupboard
I reach for it and salt my body with it
As if I were to cook myself, or bake in the oven.

Maybe then, osmosis will fail & I will shrink.

j.t (@nefarious.psyche via instagram)

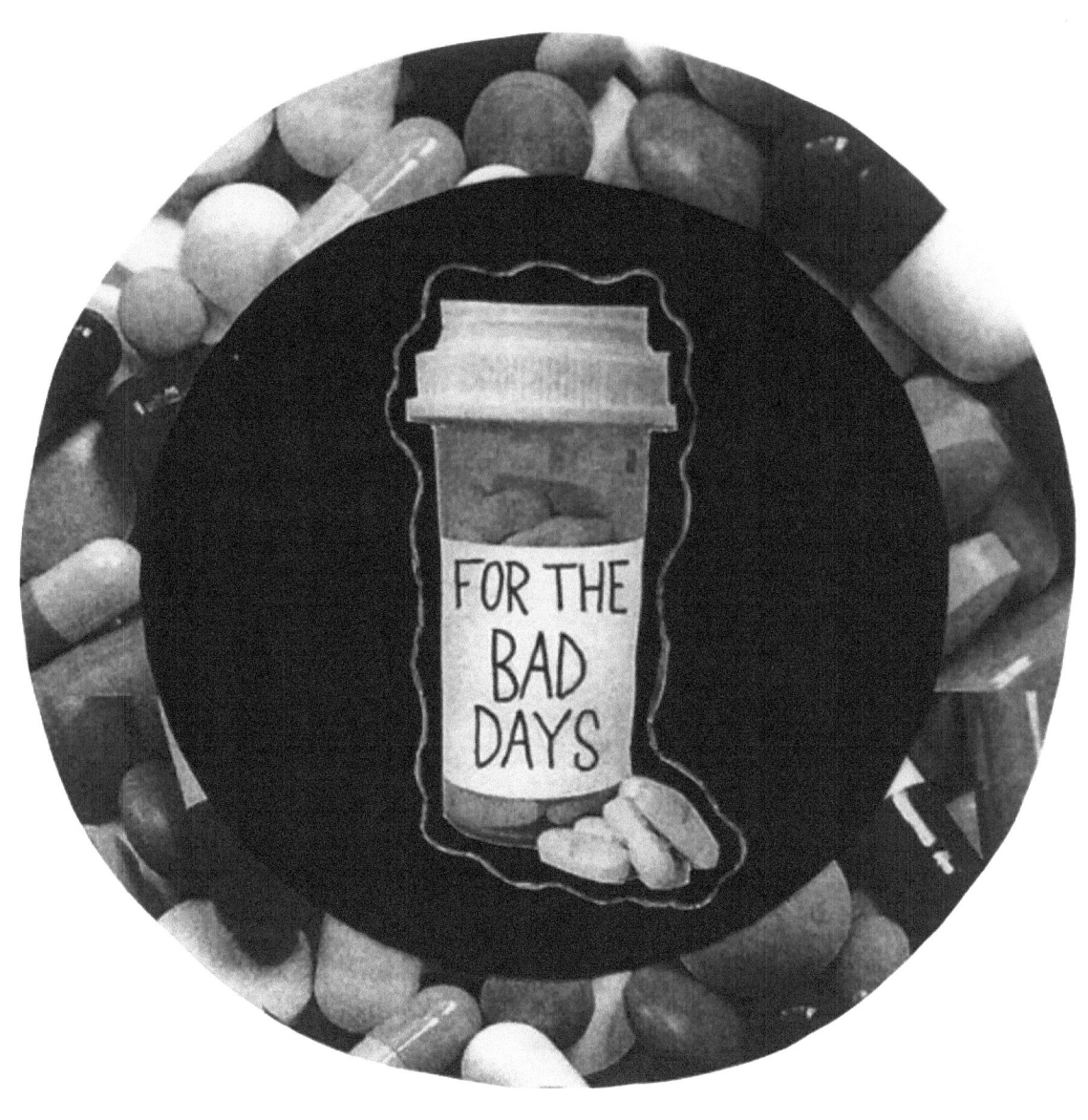

@bbsartwork

anxiety is a wild thing.

squirming inside a chest
that tightens if it senses
any kind of danger.
(or none at all)

it is earthquake hands
and accepting concrete plans
will crumble at both feet.

a choice:
to acknowledge all unbearable moments
come to an end,
even a wild thing must rest eventually.

@rainbow__ink

How do I explain
Why I am afraid
Of something so gentle?
It's just
Your smile
Is enough to make me forget
About the smiles
Before yours
That painted all these scars
And that
Is something to fear

@stones_poetry

attacks, for God's sake! He's just asking for a helping hand, but you're all too selfish, too scared to help a man in need. This is not a shameful thing, when will you realise?'

At that moment, something happened and I felt a flash of energy going through my body, accompanied with rage. As a member of this judgemental, bullying and pretentious society, I feel disgusted and ashamed. I just want to scream a couple of things from the top of my lungs, but I rather yell in my closed mind.

'ARE YOU OUT OF YOUR MINDS, THIS GUY NEED HELP; HE NEEDS HELP BECAUSE OF YOU. HE'S AFRAID OF FAILURE BECAUSE SEVERE PUNISHMENT IS ALL HE EVER KNEW. HE DOESN'T WANT TO DISAPPOINT ANYONE, SO HE KEEPS DISAPPOINTING HIMSELF INSTEAD. HE DOESN'T TELL YOU ABOUT HIS PASSIONS AND ALL THE THINGS HE LOVES TO DO BECAUSE HE'S AFRAID OF YOUR JUDGEMENT. CAN'T YOU SEE HOW MUCH THAT SCARES HIM? HOW IT SHATTERS HIM TO BITS? IT ALL TERRIFIES SO MUCH THAT HE DOESN'T EVEN DARE TO THINK ABOUT WHAT WOULD YOU DO IF YOU FOUND OUT ABOUT ALL OF IT, THAT HE FREEZES AND FAINTS FROM MENTAL EXHAUSTION YOU PUT UPON HIS INNOCENT, KIND MIND. YOU DID THIS!

WHAT IS WRONG WITH YOU PEOPLE, CAN'T YOU SEE ALL THE HUMAN BEINGS ON THIS PLANET ARE AT LEAST A LITTLE MENTAL? ADMIT IT TO YOURSELVES AT ONCE; WE ALL HAVE MENTAL ISSUES OF A KIND.'

As I do not dare to say those things out loud, I stand there heartbroken as I walk past all those cruel, inhumane spectators and make my way to the terrified, shocked man on the floor. I offer him my hand, and when he takes it, I take him into my arms.

"Shhh, it's alright. Don't worry, you are not alone in this. Not anymore, not ever — I know exactly how, and what you feel."

I lean even closer to his ear so that nobody else could ever hear me saying:

"I suffer from these, too. I know how bad it can get, but you're not alone anymore. I am here for you, and always will be."

He rocks back and forth in my embrace; as a matter of fact, we rock together, collided on the floor. People around us disappear, and as he looks straight into my eyes, I know I've gained the young man's trust. I take his hand in mine and make us both stand. We stand up tall, high and strong, as I turn around and quietly say:

"Thank you for making us a spectacle worth watching," and lead the man out of this social trap for falling, mentally unstable prey.

j.t (@nefarious.psyche via instagram)

I walked to a bus stop in the cold, thin air.

I stood there and I waited.

I waited and the world captured my muse.

It seemed to be at as much a loss of pace as me.

A paradox of infinite serenity.

Frozen. Lost. Just lost.

A far off constellation in outer space,

Where the end of time is an obscure concept,

Where the end of time is nothing but a myth

And endings are only in the fabric of fairy tales.

For you and I, we tend to be racing

And the place we inhabit tends to stay eternal.

It never changes.

I blinked and I saw a tram charging at me.

The bubble of calm took away the immediacy of the situation.

It's wheels running rapid like a high waterfall.

You don't see the water, falling down in patches of blue.

You only feel the strength.

I saw. I did see.

Yet, I felt nothing.

How easy is it to die?

That was my first thought.

How easy it is to die

When the chariot from hell is mere metres away

To bring you your fate.

It is easy.

It is very easy.

How easy is it for me to die?

That was what I thought next.

All I have to do is stay rooted to my spot.

To do this thing of immense value,

All I have to do ***is nothing.***

Just stand there with a firm faith

And be ready to acknowledge my fate.

The tram came and I let it pass me by.

I took a step back and once again I saw,

The face of the driver and the people inside,

Plain oblivious to the workings of my mind.

I stepped back and I saw.

The bubble burst away.

Rapid commotion,

Vibrant insolation

Found its way

Back into my day.

So, I guess,

It'll be okay

And I'll be fine

For one more day.

@inebriating_society

When the 'what ifs'
become your only
thoughts,
a mind that once
soared above
the clouds
now drifts
into the abyss
of insecurity
that both you and I
have forced upon me.

Anxiety,
a sheep in
wolves' clothing
crying into the
daylight
that we have
mistaken for
darkness.

When our only
options are
fight or flight,
we choose
to destroy
ourselves
every
time.

- shepherd's play

by Anna Maria Hanna (@ampoetry_)

I don't want to tell you

lately I don't know what's going on inside of my head. sometimes I would just get off from work and just sit there. I don't feel like talking to anyone. I don't even want to be by myself, but I don't even know how I'm feeling. sometimes it feels like I don't deserve you. sometimes I don't feel like being positive, sometimes I want to let the negative energy grow into something that's still worth the pain. I know that it can be depressing talking to me, I know that I preach the lightness of the day way too much to be this sad. but if you felt a little bit better, maybe my existence means something.

maybe that's my problem. I'd die for you, probably even let you kill me. if happiness comes with a cost, I'd let you take it all away. from the cornerstones of the music ringing in my skull— the sad songs pull me towards a bitter end. I'm full of flaws and writing poetry is just another way to pass the time. maybe that's why i write so much to sad people. they all need answers that they think I can give, the irony. i wish that my arms can hold the weight of it all. inside a tiny ball of fire, my heart sleeps. inside of this pale blue dot, my soul weeps.

sometimes I wake up and I'm disappointed because her parents were right and she was right to leave me. I'm worth nothing. I don't know how to look at you and tell you that everything is going to be alright for me. I don't know how to tell you that I still think about her or possibly even love someone I no longer know. from sundown to sunrise. sometimes I wonder if I was ever going to be good enough for anyone. and that's why I withdraw from people so often. a poor excuse for a life. but life is given, we were dealt an impossible task of living and waking up to find some sort of normality in mundane day to day tasks. sometimes I wake up and I don't want to live. I shrug it off. but it comes back. and as I'm faced with the reality of living like this is no different than just outright dying, I'm afraid. afraid that they were right and that I'll never be shit because I'm not shit and I'll never be able to live up to who they think i should be. but in truth— I don't even know who I am, much less who i should be in this life. it's sad because it's true. it's fucked up because it's real. when we die, we all die the same. no one knows what happens after life. and sometimes it makes me sad that if i died right now, I'd hurt so many people.

i know that it's hard to see me like this, but it's the things that I don't talk about that you notice the most. I notice you noticing those little details. when I don't make you feel appreciated, it's because I'm forgetful. chasing after a high that I won't have again. sometimes I'm afraid that we'll have the same ending. if love is the answer to everything, then why am I so hard on myself? I tell people to love themselves, but I haven't even started. the path to loving yourself isn't easy. it's a day to day grind that'll remind you of how unimportant you are if you just disappeared right now.

I've tried to be a pillar of hope for lost souls, but I found out real soon that it's just the blind leading the blind. I can't fix their problems with a thousand love poems, it's all just glitter and stardust. inside of my heart it still feels hurt. on the outside it still looks fine I guess. the occasional thought that I'll be fine is just that. maybe I will. maybe I won't. a small factor in my daily routines. I don't know why I try to help so many people. maybe it makes me feel good. maybe I feel bad because I've been there and done that. but if you keep picking at a wound, it won't heal properly. maybe I help people because I want them to feel like it's okay. there's hope. and maybe there is. sometimes I just don't think there is any left for me once I've written it all out.

lately I've been everywhere. I enter a meditative state while it rains and I'm in love with that natural feeling like I should be watching the rain as it falls down. but I also sit there and think about all of the tears that I've caused. all of the pain that I've left there. without a word. sometimes I want to just scream until I am no more. words trickling in the blood, my eyes are too blurry with the salt, my stars too hidden by the city lights, my constellations do hear my woes, for when the night comes I am my only foe. my only enemies are my thoughts. I keep myself tied to my depression like it's my only way to function. inside of the clouds, I make friends with the rain. somewhere with the bees, I feel the petals. the deep honey roasted glaze on your eyes kissing the sun with a wink— it reminds me of who I need to be. I often tell people to let things happen day by day and if it gets ugly, just brush it off. start anew. I never tell them that it's hard to do because I want them to have faith and hope in the universe. sometimes I don't know how to tell you that I'm scared that love won't last. sometimes I'm scared to tell you that I'm not feeling good because that would mean that you'd try to cheer me up. and I don't want to disappoint you yet again, so I do a little laugh. and maybe that's the answer to all of my questions— to give it a try even if you're not up for it. maybe that's the trick to being alive. I don't want to just live and exist. I'm tired of buying shit that i don't need and dumping drugs into my body or polluting my lungs with nicotine. i wake up everyday with fear. fear of everything is fine, but fear of yourself is never a good thing. because how can you go on living if you're afraid of being yourself? it's so damn funny to me— the fact that i love hating myself more than i actually should hate hating myself. cruelty to the human body will fade, but self-induced depression is by far the scariest thing I've ever had to experience and I don't know how to not be like this.

sometimes I wake up and I feel fine.

darling, today is not one of those days.

@pianoetry & @teacup13

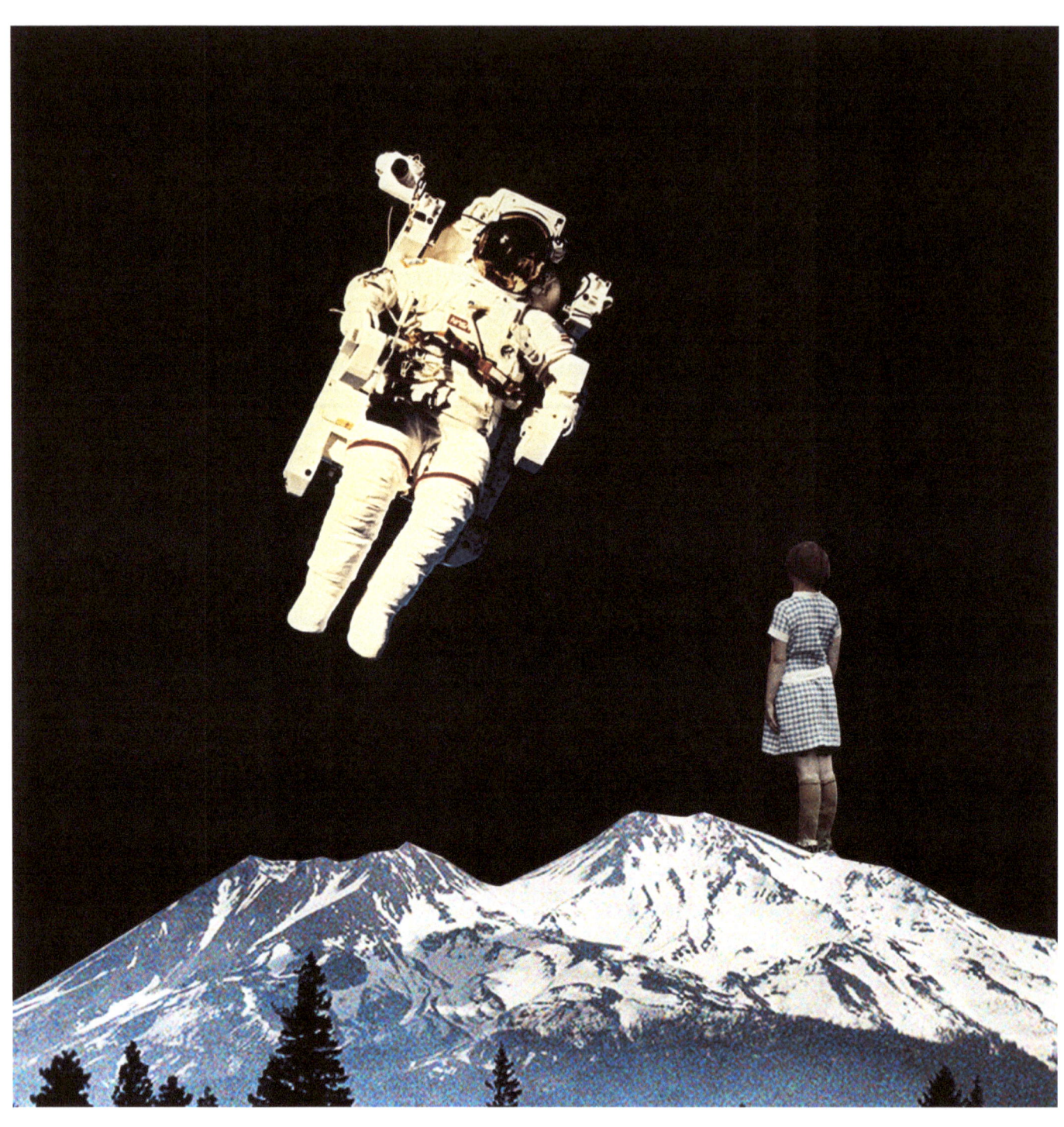

@iridesenceofbeing

I'm listening to Saturn by Sleeping At Last
While my eyes start to water
My thoughts go back to the last 12 months
And how at the very beginning
I wanted to leave this world
I could have never resembled the lyrics
Even though I thought there was something worth living for
But I hadn't found it then
So I gave up my search too soon
But there has always been a piece of hope in my heart
That wasn't willing to go and leave
A small glimpse of light
That almost burned down

Now I'm here
And I'm surprised
That I am still here
That I am still alive
That I still walk this Earth
That I love more than I have imagined
I'm here
My heart is beating
My body is working
My brain is dreaming
I'm living
All that has always been a fantasy of mine
I had thought of this
While writing my suicide letter
Now the life before this year is just a nightmare of my past
I'm crying
But I'm crying of how unbelievable it is to find myself happy, sorrow free, recovered, loved, enthusiastic ... alive.

@sandyplottke

Biographies

@adisorderedmind_zines: Is currently living in London, UK with her partner and their much loved cat. A fairly new zinester, She uses the zine making processes as a therapeutic and self expressive activity. Many of her zines focus on mental illness, including anxiety, depression and BPD, or share personal life experiences from dealing with grief to coming out in a religious environment.

@ampoetry_: Anna Maria is an emerging Australian poet of Coptic heritage. She shares excerpts of her original poetry as well as musings on her Instagram, @ampoetry_. Her pieces make commentary on topics such as body positivity, mental health & healing, self – love, womanhood/girlhood, feminism, friendship, and vulnerability.

@annaxmania: She married all her manias/ It was sad to watch / good reception though

@artful_agony: Artful agony distracts herself from an endless parade of unexplainable symptoms by making art. She lives in Sydney, Australia. You can find her work at www.artfulagony.com, or on Instagram @artful_agony.

@art_has_feeling: Why do words have to be the only way to help you understand?

@artyprose: Hello I'm Jesa, just another wandering soul. But I hope I could find my place soon and I hope the same for you.

@bbsartwork: Is currently a full time student in her third year of university studying fine art and illustration. She has Tourette's syndrome, anxiety, and depression. She uses art to express how her conditions make her feel, which helps her better deal with them.

@bipolarbear_art: As I pursue a degree in social work, my love of art has allowed me to explore and share my experience with mental health.

@colette.lh: Colette Love Hilliard is a writer and teacher whose book A Wonderful Catastrophe traces her journey of love, marriage, and infertility through poetry and art.

@drixkie: Is a freelancer and a mom. She's undiagnosed, but has been suffering from anxiety and depression since she was 11. She's still learning how to be a proper person.

@floretstars: Taylor is an 18 year-old amateur writer whose goal is to overcome the word 'can't and drink a lot of coffee while doing it.

@_firevalley_: Alessandra is a psychology student from Italy. She likes to define herself as an artist, because she's loved every form of art for her whole life, and throughout the years, art has helped her express herself.

@just-4-thought: In the second grade, Meg wrote her first anthology series. She discovered characters, plots, and entire worlds at the tips of her fingers. When her classmates began writing fanfiction with her characters, she picked up the pencil and never looked back. Since then, her writing career has taken her from murder mysteries dinner parties to Capitol Hill, but by far one of her favorite places is right here in the writing community. The friendship and support are unparalleled. Writing can take us anywhere together.

@morethanmagnets: morethanmagnets is a 25 year old who enjoys spending time with her cat, her lovely boyfriend, and her magnets. She is a language nerd, a crafter, and likes to play Hedbanz with her students.

@my_troubled_art: Is a self taught author and artist that grew up on all types of fantasy stories; and he uses that experience to navigate the chaos of his heart to show others that they can see the beauty in his pain.

@nefarious.psyche: J.T is a young poetess and creative soul with aspiring career as an activist writer. She is striving towards voices being heard and tackles issues that are often not spoken about. You can read more of her work on Instagram at @nefarious.psyche

@inebriating_sobriety

@iridescenceofbeing

@_ohmycas: Casandra Rojas is a passionate Venezuelan writer whose poetry focuses on the human condition, and transmitting raw emotion through lyrical wordplay.

@pi.and.anne: Kati Mohr, born 1976 is an intuitive writer going with the flow, artist and designer of all things including yarn, pens & paper, and believes in creativity as a strong force and bonding that we all share because of our diversity and uniqueness. She also loves math and strawberries in chocolate.

@pianoetry: and after all that I've seen, I still believe in love.

@rainbow__ink: Abigail Zerr is a 20 year old poet in Edmonton, Alberta. Her writing sheds light on the importance of mental health and self-care. She's been published in the magazine called "Growth". She hopes to release a collection of poetry in the future.

@redlightwriting

@robertjw4688: Robert J. W. is a writer, digital artist, and photographer from Morgantown, WV. He enjoys listening to music, watching videos, nature walks, and video games.

@roman—empyre

@sandyplottke: Sandy is a German-Polish writer that has been dealing with depression, anxiety, and OCD for half her life. Through social media and writing she tries helping others and spreading awareness about mental illnesses.

@stones_poetry: Stones Poetry is a young woman of 21 living in the South East of the UK. Her inspiration comes from past relationships and the friends around her. She is planning to publish a debut poetry book in 2020.

@storieslikestars: Nicole Gusto is passionate about her day job as a therapist in the rehabilitation sector, but she is also a huge geek for stories. She loves using words to speak life to readers. You can find more of her work at https://nicolgeusto.com and https://onevoicemagazine.com.